# How to Write a Strong Busines

Karen Cherrett

First Published 2017.

Revised 2020.

ISBN: 978-1-365-75127-1

projectmanagementinsight.com

# Table of Contents

# A message to you

Is your project idea valid? Would running a project now, be viable? Those are the questions that you want to be able to answer when you write a business case.

This book has been written for you, the business case writer. Whether this is the first time you are writing one, or you have written many before I hope you gain value from reading it.

More and more decision makers these days require a properly formulated business case to substantiate the decision to spend funds.

Projects are not projects until you receive the green light for them and in most cases, the process of receiving this 'green light', including allocation of funding, begins with a business case, or at least that is what should happen.

Organisations waste time and money by handing over funds for projects with minimal substantiation of the business outcome. By this, I mean what the business benefit of spending these funds is.

For existing businesses, the business case will lead into a full blown project, but for new businesses, it will result in the preparation of a business plan.

In my experience, many people struggle with how to write a good strong business case. The process may not be something that you have undertaken before, and so you have no idea where to start, or what is even needed. There are templates you can use, with headings, but you have no real idea what is required, regarding content. By you having a strong understanding of the type and depth of information needed you will be able to pull together a strong business case that shows that the project idea is viable.

This book is the beginning of an education process to assist you, the business case writer, to understand how to find and put together the right information to build your strong business case.

It contains some useful tips that will assist you. Other key points are also called out in blue text.

Having read many business cases during my twenty years of working life, I notice that people struggle with what makes a business case strong and viable. The business cases I have written have been praised for the quality information contained in them.

I want to share my knowledge and insights with you so you can understand how to write a strong, viable business case too.

This book is the first in a series that will detail each of the key areas on running successful projects. In my opinion, so many projects fail because they are missing this key foundation document: a well-written business case. Without it – an absolute chance of project failure. With it – a better chance of project success.

Which path will you choose? I am hoping that by purchasing this book, you are choosing the latter.

# 1. Introduction

A business case is a key document for any project. It is the beginning of the beginning, for without a business case you do not get the funding, people, time or whatever else it is that you need to make the change you are seeking, be that within your organisation, or in setting it up.

All change initiatives, no matter what form they take should begin with a business case; justification for why this change is needed.

Without it, you do not have management support to undertake the change needed, be that the build of a system, the implementation of a strategy, or the setting up of a program of work. With it, you have the right level of buy-in and understanding about the desired change and its benefits.

### Writing the business case

Many people come to writing business cases for the first time with little knowledge of what a business case is, the need for it, and what information it should contain. Others have written many business cases and fall into the same traps over and again – resulting in poorly formulated projects.

Many people do not have the background knowledge of the organisation or area they are working in to gather the right information, let alone the right level of information. Alternatively, they have worked in the area for many years and are buried in the detail of day-to-day operations and are not necessarily able to see the bigger picture.

The key to a good and sound business case is **to gather the necessary level of information based on reality and facts** for inclusion.  The aim when writing is to include the right level of detail so that as the project is delivered, there are no surprises.

This book provides details and a set of tips that will assist you in gathering the information so that your business case is strong and your sponsor or signatories can make a decision based on the detail it contains.

It will help set out the **why** you need what you are proposing to happen and **what** it is that is required to achieve the desired business outcome.

> Business cases are required for all sorts of reasons in business. They are a critical decision-making document.

For me, the process of writing a business case is not linear. Once you start following the steps outlined you are gathering information all the time for the different sections of your business case. You will notice items for the various parts coming up. To write a business case well, you need to be immersed in it and thinking all the time about how the information you are being given can be used.

Start thinking risks, and benefits from the moment you start your information gathering process. Capture items or tasks that need to be carried out in a draft project plan. This level of detail is not required for your high-level timeline, and it will save time when the project gets the go ahead.

Keep a running log of key material that you are being told or provided. This list will be valuable in helping complete your assumptions section.

A well-produced business case will simplify the decision-making process as well as provide you (in whatever role you occupy) with much-needed information to determine if the reasons for moving forward with a project are sound.

> A well-written business case will assist in determining if there is value continuing with a project or stopping it before it gets started. There is no wasted time in producing a good business case.

Keep this book handy and revisit the tips as a reminder every time you are putting together a new business case.

If you have previously written business cases, you might find this book useful in assessing the level of information that you have written already, and whether there are changes you can make to add more value to your business cases moving forward.

## 2. What is a Business Case?

A Business Case is the fundamental starting point,
for any project or business plan.

Let's go back to basics for a moment.

Here are a few definitions of the word 'case.'

- ◈ The Oxford English Dictionaries – "an instance of a particular situation; an example of something occurring.  An instance of a disease, injury, or problem."

- ◈ Chambers 21st Century Dictionary – "a particular occasion, situation or set of circumstances.  A matter requiring investigation."

- ◈ The Encyclopaedic World Dictionary – "a state of things involving a question for discussion or decision."

Therefore, in the context of a business case, your aim is to produce a document fully describing the current situation and what you see you need to resolve the problem or take up the opportunity that exists.

It is written to create clarity and gain agreement to commit an allocation of funding, and resources, to undertake a project, with the outcome of making a valuable change for the organisation.

This commitment of financing will be based on a thorough understanding of what is going to be achieved for the business, as the outcome of the spending. Some examples are:

- we will recruit five additional staff

- we will purchase and implement a new CRM system

- we will fully automate a manual process allowing staff to focus on other core tasks.

The decision to allocate funds is ultimately made based on the strength of the detailed information that is provided in your business case document and presentation.

It is important that you provide <u>enough</u> quality information for your sponsor or delegate to be able to make a reasoned decision and understand at a high-level what the project will look like to deliver the change.

I suggest that you use the headings I provide in this book to give your decision makers information in the key areas they will be looking for:

- They need to understand what the problem is you want to solve

- Alternatively, the opportunity that you want to take up

- Why you want the funds and resources, you are requesting

- What options are available to deliver this business change

- The benefits to the business of making this change

- Key risks involved and how will they be mitigated

- What will implementing this change cost

- The projected timeline for completion of the change

- What assumptions are you making in putting this information together

- Your recommendation for moving forward

Once you have gathered the information in each of these areas, it will be clear if your business case 'stacks up', or not.

The business case itself does not need to be a large document. Its size will depend on the scale of the change. What is important is that it contains the right level of information in an easy to read manner.

I have spoken about the 'right level' of information several times now.  What do I mean by that?  For me the right level of information means providing enough information that I could, without any prior knowledge at all about the business, its functions or systems, read what I have been provided and make a clear and supported decision to approve funds for this project.

Many times I see business cases that are tombs thick, and yet a lot of the key and critical information for sound decision making is missing.

The information must stand alone.  It must be supported and self-contained.

We will look at each of the key elements that make up a business case in the following pages.

## 3. Understand your audience

The first place to start, before you do any writing, is to understand who your key stakeholders are. Understanding them is a valuable step and one that has saved me many times when preparing business cases.

Ask yourself these questions

'Who are the people most interested in this business case?'

'Who will be reading it to validate the change(s) I am suggesting?'

You might also consider who might lose if this opportunity is not taken up, or the problem not fixed? Who has responsibility for signing off the funds and resources you require?

Understanding your audience is a valuable step in determining the needs of your audience.

## Who are your key stakeholders or signatories?

Each key stakeholder or signatory will require something different from the information in your business case. There is value in understanding what it is that they are wanting.

For example your Chief Financial Officer (CFO) will likely focus on the Return on Investment (ROI) figure contained in your financial analysis, whereas the General Manager of Operations will want to see the benefits from the efficiency gains spelled out and how that may relate to dollar savings to his area.

If you understand key stakeholder needs, you have a better chance of obtaining support for the signoff of your Business Case. Canvas each key stakeholder and ask them what they will need to see in your document for them to support it.

## Whom are the people required to help you in writing your business case?

Have you got a clear picture of the individuals or teams who will need to be involved in providing you with information and cost estimates for your Business Case? This pre-writing time is the time to ask questions and ensure that once you understand your end to end process, that you have all the key people captured and involved in one role or another.

A Responsibility Assignment Matrix (RACI) may be valuable to document whom you have spoken to and their role in the Business Case development and, if approved, the project moving forward. A RACI will also allow you to highlight areas where you do not have the desired level of information for your business case development.

Here is what the information in a RACI matrix represents. It names the people or group you are interacting with and what their level of involvement is based on these definitions.

*[R] Responsible* The person or persons who are responsible for the outcome. This will usually be the Project Manager or may be the Project Sponsor.

*[A] Accountable* The person whose job it is to complete the task. That may be you, or someone else who is supporting you with information gathering for the business case.

**[C] Consulted** Those whose opinions you gather. These are typically subject matter experts. You will continue to gather information and question them during the life of building your business case.

**[I] Informed** People whose opinions you gather and who are kept in the loop regarding what is happening. These may be people who may be impacted by the outcome of the project, and yet not directly.

By completing a RACI matrix you are assisting with the assumption area of your business case. When key signatories are looking at this matrix they will be able to identify key people or areas that need to be involved, if they haven't been.

### Setting up your relationships

By establishing the relationship with the major stakeholders up front, and understanding where their interests lie, you are gaining critical buy-in for your business case, even before you start writing it.

They may provide you with valuable information (that you may otherwise not find), and become your advocate for championing your business case through to approval and sign-off.

They may also advise you of key people that need to be approached who hold vital information that must be considered as part of your business case development.

It is important to have established your relationships with all of the principal signatories for your business case before getting too far into writing it.

<u>Do Not</u> leave it till the week before your business case requires approval to make contact with your key stakeholders or signatories.

Consider people that you will want on your business case review panel.  These may or may not be in addition to your key stakeholders.  It is important to have a group of people knowledgeable about the business as part of your review process.  They should have sufficient knowledge of the firm to understand if you are missing any key elements and to validate your assumptions.

They should be people who are open-minded enough to consider the change being proposed.  While the change may impact them in a negative way, if they are open to it, it will make implementing the change associated with the business case easier.

Having buy-in for the change is another valuable reason for this relationship building early on in your business case development process, as it will make project implementation easier should your business case be approved.

## TIP 1 – KNOW YOUR AUDIENCE

Do your groundwork in setting up your relationships with the major decision makers who will evaluate and approve your Business Case. Ensure that the information you provide meets their needs and gives them the confidence to support the project moving forward.

# 4. Do some digging, ask some questions

There are two key aspects to the investigatory work required that are both important and play a role in how complete, or otherwise, your business case ends up.

**Understand your current business practices**

The first critical area that is often overlooked when writing a business case is the analysis of the current business practices.

Who knows the impacted business systems and processes inside out?  Sometimes identifying these people is not easy, but the value in finding them is that they will then not be the people who, 2/3rds of the way through your project tell you that what you are suggesting won't work.  Not having this total view of the current business practices is something that creates project failure.

The people you are looking for are the detail oriented ones, those with hands-on experience of the day to day operations of the business.  Alternatively, they may be people who have been in the business area for many years and have the full working knowledge of what has happened previously, as well as what currently happens during the day to day operations.

By finding and working with these people now in the initial phase of developing your project, you will gain much-needed buy-in for the change management aspects. These people can quickly become your change advocates due to their early engagement.

One of the fundamental problems that I see with many projects is that the individual writing the business case does not fully understand the current business practices in such a way that means they can be wary of anything that doesn't 'feel' right in the business case development journey.

What do I mean by this? If you are writing the business case and someone provides you with information that you have an instinct doesn't match either the current business process, or what you think it should be, then you will instinctively seek our more information.

If you are not involved enough in the business outcome, you will not have this instinct and therefore write from an outsiders perspective, which could mean not questioning or evolving something that needs to be considered.

## Who needs to be involved in the information gathering?

The second key aspect of this information gathering phase is who needs to be involved. You may shy away from talking to people that you think have a strong opinion about this project going ahead, especially if they consider it will adversely affect them.

You may also not understand the full end to end process and as such who each of the people at the touch points are. It's important to ask the questions and find the contacts. These people will provide you will valuable insights that will help you strengthen your case.

Remember, the key in looking at who to talk to is risk mitigation. If you speak to the right people up front, before you get into the detailed writing, you are already starting to understand the risks involved in going ahead with this project. This is very valuable.

Once you have identified the key people that need to be involved in assisting you with the information gathering, it is worthwhile asking if business processes have been mapped and are available.

These may prove invaluable in your option development, and assumption statement building.

What may be required at this point in the process is that a documented set of Business Requirements are produced.

I will always advocate for documented Business Requirements versus not having them.

The time that you save in producing them and using them to help define the content of your business case is invaluable.

Again, including this process in your development creates a stronger chance of project success, based on my years of experience, watching the projects without them fail.

Documented business requirements help to set out the scope of what will be delivered.  Scope creep in projects is costly. Setting the project parameters and working to deliver within those parameters should be the aim of your business case.

### What's the History?

Ask people within the business who have worked in the area for some time if the organisation has considered and visited this problem or opportunity before and if so was a business case prepared.

Try to source a copy of earlier developed material, especially if it was not approved.

Try to find out why it was not approved previously. Ask if the people in the business know why this was the case.  Asking these question will provide you gather useful information about what may have been lacking or what options are not worth considering, and why.  It might also show you avenues to investigate due to changes that have occurred in the organisation or context since that time.

By obtaining a copy of the previously prepared material, you might also find that most of the work that you need has already been completed for you and that you might only need to review an earlier version and update the financial estimates

I do not advocate using old versions of a Business Case and only updating the financial information contained in it though.  Only updating this information is a recipe for disaster. Review each section of the already written business case against the material in this guide, to validate if the business case stacks up.

## Taking a fresh look at what's gone before

Through reading this book, it might become apparent to you why the earlier version of the business case was not approved. Take what you learn from this book, and look at the previous material with fresh eyes.

If you see that it is not worthwhile updating an earlier business case, then make the decision to start again with the knowledge that you know what is required to generate something that's strong and viable.

## Consider confidentiality, even at this early stage

Understand if there are any privacy requirements around the proposed project. Consider if there are people you should not be talking to at this early stage.

Don't go external to the organisation unless you need to. Be sure to gain a solid understanding from within the business first.

**If you are seeking advice from external third parties, consider confidentiality agreements before you go too far down the track of disclosing what you are proposing.**

This is valuable when you are gathering information from vendors who have provided a system previously, for example. You may not want them knowing what you are doing as it may mean discontinuation of their services.

It may be worthwhile getting a legal expert from your organisation involved and across what you are proposing, in case there are any issues that might arise further down the track.

**Do your research**

Take the time to do your research. Time spent at this writing stage will assist you with answering detractor questions when your business case goes up for approval.

Better to have asked a group within an organisation and had them say that they cannot assist or do not need to be involved in this project if it gets off the ground, than not ask.

If you do not engage a group that should have been involved, you are more likely to uncover critical issues with your project during project delivery, especially if that team held key information relating to your end to end process and you were not aware of it.

You may also find you need resources from that group to deliver your project and if their estimate was not included in your business case, your project manager might not have the resources available when they need them.

---

## TIP 2 – DO YOUR RESEARCH

*Valuable time spent researching will show you key factors to be included or used, may stop rework, or allow you to understand why a previous business case was not successful.*

---

# 5. How to define your problem statement

How to succinctly describe your problem is an area that challenges many people. I will try to make it simple for you.

Firstly ask yourself, 'What is the problem that you (or the business) currently have and are working to solve?'

You need to describe this issue, succinctly, in no more than a single paragraph. What you want to do is explain the problem in such a way as to create an image in the mind of those reading it. Creating a succinct statement is not as easy as it sounds.

What I usually see here is a motherhood statement that does not go anywhere near describing the real problem. It contains lots of words and a minimal amount of factual information.

## What is the real problem?

Here is an example of what I consider a real problem statement:

*"Customer Relationship Management within the organisation is currently managed using multiple spreadsheets, with no clear history of our total client base or our interactions with them. Due to this, we are*

*unable to define who our most active customers are, and how we interact with them."*

In this example, you will see that the statement creates a picture of what the current problem looks like and its impact on the business. While it has not provided any details of the size of the problem, due to the nature of the current business process, this may not be at all possible, and for this reason, the benefits of making the change may not be known.

Note the key points:

- CRM is managed using multiple spreadsheets

- No clear history of the client base

- No clear history of the interactions with clients

- No ability to define the most active customers

- No ability to determine how we interact with the most active customers

Notice that this statement does not describe the benefits of what is going to be achieved. It does not explain why this needs to be done or done a certain way. It is very clear though in describing the current problem that exists.

When a key stakeholder or signatory reads this, they would be able to clearly see in their mind what this business case is trying to do, what problem it is seeking to solve.

Using this example, they would want the business case to show them HOW this project is going to fix this issue of managing client data relating to interactions with the company's most active customers.

This problem statement can also be considered an elevator pitch. Elevator pitches need to be short, and succinct.  They need to describe something that can be pictured and easily understood by the person hearing it. A problem statement is no different.

What should occur when your stakeholders or signatories read your problem statement is they should have a picture of what the problem is in their mind. If they won't get this clear picture from what you've written, keep working on it.

**Include statistics if you have them**

It is important to include statistics in your statement if they are available and relevant. Note my use of the word 'relevant' here.  Don't include them just for the sake of it. You want the statistics to add value and clarity to your problem statement.

Remember, when your sponsor or delegate reads the problem statement, they should be able to see the problem themselves and fully understand it. Keep it simple.

What you are aiming to do is create a picture of the person reading this statement, something they can clearly see, or understand from your words.

**Ask the following questions once you have drafted a statement:**

◈ Am I clear about the problem we are trying to solve and do I have a precise definition written down?

◈ Do I need to be a member of the impacted business area to understand this documented problem statement?

Writing a problem statement that does not require a degree of inside business knowledge to understand its meaning is important. If your statement cannot be understood by anyone reading it, then the statement may need to be revised as there is an assumed amount of knowledge that is required to read it.

Formulate your problem statement for someone that knows nothing about the area or the problem you are defining. This way you can be sure that it is as clear as it needs to be.

Remember, no jargon or acronyms. You are writing it for a stranger.

An unclear problem statement leads to confusion around your case for change. A clearly written problem statement is an essential first step to documenting your Business Case.

> The problem statement shapes the scope of your project. It is important that it be defined in a way that creates clarity.

### Don't rush this process

Spending time explaining the real problem succinctly, in your problem statement is of immeasurable value to the proposed project

Note my words "the _real_ problem." A problem statement is not about the problem that people 'think' exists.

The only way to sit and understand the real problem begins with gaining an understanding of the business processes. What is currently happening? What is it that we want to do and are unable to, and why?

By looking at things this way, it will usually highlight a gap in the process or systems capability. By seeing this, you are then starting to understand what the problem is and where it exists.

Start by getting a group of relevant business people in a room and brainstorm what they know about the problem. Write down the key points that they are highlighting. This brainstorming will begin to give you a flavour of the current situation and where the pain points are for the business.

From this, you will then be able to piece together, through listening, what those in the company see the problem as. Remember, it is not going to be the same as what these staff are telling you is necessarily happening.

The business team will be giving you the details of their day to day work, what is and is not going on. The day to day process is not the problem. The problem is what is not going on, what they are not getting from doing their work, what is missing in the process. What is missing or not working is key, and often where problem statements become not well defined.

Draft one statement and put it out to the group for review. Let people have time to sit and see if the statement describes their understanding of the problem.

What you will find by following this process is that things are identified which will allow you to start to understand scoping of your project. For example, this problem definition process will begin to highlight other things that will be considered out of scope for your project. It may also highlight key things that need to be included.

Using our example problem statement above, we need to define if we are talking about ALL of our x million customers or only clients of a particular product type.

Looking at our problem statement this way allows us to notice that if we are talking about our entire client base. If we are, then this would be a larger project than only for those customers of a particular product.

Taking this view makes it possible to ask questions to define the problem and therefore the scope.

# 6. How to define your opportunity statement

The key reason for needing your business case might be that an opportunity has presented itself.  For this, you need to write an opportunity statement

The statement itself needs to be clear as previously described for the problem statement. The questions that you ask to help determine the opportunity are a little different, however.

Consider these questions to write your opportunity statement:

◈ How would you succinctly describe this opportunity?

◈ What does the organisation gain?

◈ Why would you want to take it up right now, or at some other time in the future?

◈ What is the benefit of taking it up right now?

Be clear and succinct about the opportunity.  Be sure to describe the benefits to the organisation in a statistical manner if possible as part of your statement.

An opportunity statement might look like this:

*"Visitors to Melbourne have trouble understanding where to purchase a public transport ticket. The opportunity is to produce an application that would allow visitors with a smartphone to pinpoint the closest convenience store from which to purchase a ticket with the aim of obtaining a 25% increase in additional purchases in store from these visitors."*

Notice that this opportunity statement does contain information on why it is important to take up this opportunity. The benefits information in the business case should clearly show WHY there is a need to increase the purchase of tickets within convenience stores.

Use the tips and ideas included in the area about developing a problem statement. They are as relevant for an opportunity statement.

Write a draft opportunity statement and test it with people within the organisation. If they can clearly repeat back to you what it is that you are trying to achieve with this project, your statement is clear enough.

If they can't, then continue to refine and reframe it.

Remember, the requirement is to create a picture for the reader that is clear.

---

*TIP 3 – BE SURE YOUR PROBLEM OR OPPORTUNITY STATEMENT IS CLEAR*

*Your problem or opportunity statement needs to explain in a simple and easy to understand way for a stranger reading it, what the problem or opportunity is that you are trying to solve and what the measurable benefits are.*

---

# 7. The Do's and Don'ts of defining a Problem or Opportunity statement

**DO**

- create a simple statement that describes your problem or opportunity.

- define the real problem, not your story about it.

- allow other people to read your draft statement to validate if it is clear for them. Ask them to read your statement and tell you what they see as the problem or opportunity you are writing about.

- write the statement for a stranger with no knowledge of the business.

- include statistical information if it is available and enhances clarity of the problem.

- hold a brainstorming session to capture what is currently happening in the business to weed out what the problem is not and better define what the problem is.

**DON'T**

- provide information on the history of what has and hasn't happened previously.

- describe the current business process in fine detail in the statement.

- define the solution that you want to achieve in gaining approval for your business case.

- use statistical information if it does not add value to your problem or opportunity statement.

- write a marketing brief that tries to sell your idea.

- take five minutes to write your problem or opportunity statement.

- write your problem or opportunity statement in isolation from the business knowledge holder.

## 8. Why do you want the funds or resources?

This section of the business case is likely to be completed last, once you have undertaken all of your investigation and gathered all of the information for your business case. Consider writing a draft section as you start your business case journey and revalidate what has been written once you have finished your investigatory work.

There is a well-known saying "Start with the end in mind". This is what I am advocating here.

### What do you want to achieve?

If you were to obtain what it is that your business case is seeking (i.e. funding, or resources, or both) what would you achieve? Keep this statement short and to the point.

Also, consider this as your success statement. What is it that the business would achieve by having this business case approved?

This section could be described as similar to an executive summary in a key company document. Your signatories need to understand from their reading of it, what it is that your business case is setting out to achieve; what are the measurable achievements or objectives arising from your business case. You want to have written something that makes your signatories want to keep reading to understand the detail contained in the remainder of your business case document.

## Clearly describe the outcome

If **you** are clear about your intended outcome, it will make it easier for you to see if you have provided the right level of information to your stakeholders, for them to approve your business case. What is it that you will deliver to the business through undertaking this project?

Let's use the example from our problem statement section to show you what this would look like:

*"We will provide the business with a CRM system that will allow them to track customer interactions."*

Notice that we are not saying how we will do this or what that solution or system will look like, only what it is that we want to achieve through delivering this project. This statement is describing something tangible.  The business can see what it is that they would expect to receive by spending the funds and allocating the resources to this project.

Similarly using the opportunity statement example:

*"Development of a smartphone application that allows customers to find the nearest convenience store that sells public transport tickets."*

Notice how clear each of these statements are. They enable the reader to have a picture of exactly what they should or would be receiving for the money they spend on the project. You will also see that the statements go some way towards scope clarification.

The problem statement example is still very broad. The statement could be more specific and say the customer interactions it would include, or the business section it would provide the information for. The opportunity statement is clearer, although it could also be clearer if, for example, it included the location for the sale of public transport tickets.

I would again suggest that you have someone who does not know what you are proposing read what you have written. If that person can understand it, then there is a better chance your signatories will too. If your reader cannot understand it, then you need to work on it, until it is evident to them what you are trying to achieve.

*TIP 4 – UNDERSTAND WHAT YOU WANT AS AN OUTCOME AND ARTICULATE IT CLEARLY*

*The clearer your message here the easier it will be for your key stakeholders to make a decision to approve your business case.*

## 9. What options are available to solve your problem or create the opportunity?

A business case is for explaining your problem or opportunity and the options that you see are available to achieve the desired change via the approved project.

Options, are the ways in which you can solve the problem or opportunity, and with all things considered the best decision regarding a viable solution made.

A business case should not be written about a solution. It should not dive straight into how you are going to fix the problem or harness the opportunity based on what you think is the only way (i.e. the single solution).

Some people use a business case to argue for a favoured solution outcome, the one they believe will be the best. Writing this way is not wise as you may not have all of the facts or information available to you at the time of developing the business case.

Developing a business case to provide the sales pitch for a favourite vendors product is no benefit in the long term to the firm. Too many times I see that the ultimate solution provided not only wastes valuable time and resources, but it also goes nowhere towards fixing the real issue within the business.

As the writer of the business case, you provide options that you see are available so that your sponsor or signatories ultimately have a say in the way that the change is made.

They will make a decision based on all of the information they have at hand and can consider what will provide the best outcome for the business, both in the short and long term based on the financial outlay and the benefits.

The key to writing options is to be open minded. Consider all possibilities initially. You can always shorten your list of options when the time comes to finalise your business case.

## Brainstorm your options

One of the great ways to come up with options to include in a business case is to brainstorm them.

The best way to go about this is to decide who your knowledge experts are, those people who might help you formulate options for how you are going to solve your business problem and get them together in a room. Brief them on your problem or opportunity and ask them for their suggestions on options they see are available.

If it is not possible to get them all in a room together, find a way to gather proposals and ideas from them individually or in smaller groups. Then circulate the ideas generated to the whole group. This brainstorming could be done via email but it is not as valuable as a meeting, as people may misinterpret what you have written, and it is valuable for them to receive answers to any questions that they may have straight away.

This two way discussion also allows you to identify any issues or problems with the information you have gathered or provided; the assumptions being made and allow for questions to go back to the Business Owner of the project.

Consider virtual options for a whole group meeting. Teleconference call or video calls are invaluable in this space. Don't let distance stop you from capturing ideas from people with information about what is possible. You are aiming to get a broad perspective on what options are available to you.

It is worthwhile including a technical person (an IT architect, for instance), and an analyst and the business process owner in the room when you are brainstorming options for anything that may involve IT. I have found involving an IT architect invaluable in most circumstances at this stage.

# A method for effective brainstorming

To conduct a brainstorming session, firstly describe your problem or opportunity. Give the participants the details that you have gathered so far, and what you know about the business and its needs. Then ask them what they see as ways to solve the problem or take up the opportunity. Remember a brainstorming session is just that – there are no 'wrong ideas'. Capture (on a white board preferably) all of the ideas generated.

You might also consider approaching this session with what is known as the 'clean whiteboard' approach.

What would you do if you had no constraints, a clean slate and were starting again? This type of brainstorming might provide you with further or different ideas that are worthwhile. Ones that would not typically be considered as even possible.

Thank your participants for their input and explain that you will capture the material and distribute it for their review. Suggest that if they have any further ideas after the session to advise you.

Capture the ideas and distribute them either via a document or shared space. Provide a deadline for further input to be received. You may even consider holding a follow-up session in a few days to a weeks' time.

Once you have your list from this meeting there are a few things that you might find:-

(a) You have groupings of similar ideas that you can put together.

(b) In looking at the suggested options, you may start to see risks that are inherent in using a particular choice. Write down these risks as you notice them. If you choose to put that option in your business case, you can include these risks in your document at the same time.

(c ) You might find you have an excellent 'left field' suggestion that you would not have thought of previously, that in itself might provide the perfect option for solving your problem, or provide an easier way of taking up your opportunity.

**How many different options have you found?**

Once you have your list of options, evaluate how realistic each one is in terms of inclusion in your business case. Naturally, if you know that your sponsor only has $500,000 in his budget and you come up with something that is likely to cost $5 Million it is not going to be a valid option BUT don't let this stop you from including it. You never know what it might lead to.

Collate the brainstorm outcomes in a way that defines options for your problem or opportunity statement material.

**Consider tactical as well as strategic options**

In looking at the options that you have captured, determine if you have included both tactical and strategic ones.

Let's first look at the definition of tactical and strategic:

- The Oxford Dictionaries define **tactical** as "showing adroit planning; aiming at an end beyond the immediate action."

- The Oxford Dictionaries definition of **strategic** is "relating to the identification of long-term or overall aims and interests and the means of achieving them"

There might be a way to provide a short-term resolution to your problem or activation of your opportunity by having a tactical solution implemented. A tactical solution might mean more immediate benefits for your customers.

What might this interim solution look like?  How could or would it add value to the business if implemented now. A short-term solution can sometimes be the way to get your business case approved when it might otherwise not be.

A tactical solution might mean delivering an interim IT solution in six to 12 months rather than having to wait three or four years for the larger and more comprehensive strategic or enterprise solution to be implemented, for instance.

Sponsors or signatories always like to understand how what you are proposing will benefit the business.  If you can find a tactical solution that provides an excellent Return on Investment (ROI) or provides great value for money for the business in a not so tangible way, (for example, increases customer satisfaction), this may just be with winning factor for you in having your business case approved.

**Continually question if each option will solve the problem or opportunity that has been defined**

**Remember to include the 'Do Nothing' option**

It is important to remember there is **always** a 'Do Nothing' option. The Do Nothing option means not going ahead with anything and leaving everything exactly as it currently is.

It is important to include this in your options list so that your key stakeholders understand that they do have this option and that you have considered it.
In saying this, it is also important to point out if 'Do Nothing' ISN'T an option.

A good example of where this may not be an option is, if for legal reasons, you must change the IT system that you are using because it is currently managed by an external vendor who is going out of business, then it is certainly not a viable option to 'Do Nothing'.

By calling this out, your decision makers know that they cannot 'Do Nothing'. They then understand they must choose one of the other options that have been provided.

## Room for process improvement?

Some times in this area I see businesses who opt for an IT system to solve a problem that they have, when what would work just as well, and more cheaply is to undertake a process improvement initiative.

Consider if one of your options is to conduct a detailed process review first. While this might take time and money or resources, it may mean that the problem may be re-defined or even disappear.

It may also mean that the business may gain a benefit sooner rather than later. Your whole focus in writing this business case is to provide the business with a benefit or benefits. Is there a way to do that easily?

**What your options may look like**

After you have conducted your brainstorming session and refined your options you may come up with a list of four or five options that look something like this, using our earlier problem statement example:

Option 1. - Do Nothing: This option is to leave the business process exactly as it is and for spreadsheets to continue to be used to capture client data.  Using this solution means there will continue to be problems in identification of our most active customers and how we interact with them.

Option 2. – Purchase an 'Out of the Box' CRM system to be hosted internally:  This option would be to purchase an off the shelf CRM system, one that is specifically built for our industry. There are currently four vendors with solutions that fit the needs of the business.  Some would require customisation, others not.

Option 3. – Purchase licences for a cloud based CRM system:  This solution would allow for immediate access to a CRM system that may or may not be customisable to our specific needs.

Option 4. – Development of a purpose built CRM system: This option would see a purpose built CRM being developed. It would be possible to build a solution fully customised to the needs of the business, using the most modern technology available.

As you can see there are four different options here and each are dependent on the desired outcome that the business is wanting. They are also dependent on the funds available for the project. Each solution has different cost implications both in the short and long term. These would be spelled out in high level in your recommendation area.

# TIP 5 – REMEMBER OPTIONS NOT SOLUTIONS

Hold a brainstorming session to capture all available options. Remember to include the 'Do Nothing' option. Are there any tactical options that can be considered too?

Don't include only one solution in this area of your business case. There is always more than one way of doing something.

# 10. What are the benefits?

In compiling your business case so far I would hope that you have started to identify the benefits within the various options that you have identified. It is important to capture these and include them in your business case.

Benefits can be tangible or intangible.

Let us first look at some definitions again, to make these terms understandable.

- ◈ The Oxford Dictionaries define **Tangible** "perceptible by touch; clear and definite, real."

- ◈ They define **Intangible** as "unable to be touched, not having physical presence; difficult to define or understand, vague and abstract; (of an asset or benefit) not constituting or represented by a physical object of a value not precisely measurable."

**What are the tangible benefits for your proposed change?**

What benefits are real, clear and definite? These are the things that anyone could see or touch.

How do you measure tangible?

You measure tangible by looking at those things that you can see offer a monetary or time-saving gain for the business. You can easily substantiate them, and most likely in a way that can be included to offset the financial costs of undertaking what you are proposing.

Some examples of tangible benefits are:

- Increase sales revenue
- Reduce staff numbers when you automate a manual process
- Reduce postage due to sending documents electronically

## What are the intangible benefits of your change?

The intangible items are harder to capture, but they are just as important to consider.

An example of an intangible benefit might be that by introducing a new IT system staff are less stressed and have more time for other tasks. This feeling of being less stressed in turn may create a happier workplace.

Staff feeling less stressed could be made a tangible benefit by predicting that you would have 25% less sick days taken by staff if this system was introduced. In dollar terms, this could amount to x days sick pay not being paid out, or you might also add that there would be fewer absentee days which means that you do not require rostering of additional staff. Something you can tangibly account for from a financial perspective.

How do you tangibly account for staff happiness? That is harder to do and is not even something that needs to be accounted for, I would suggest. You might consider that a happier workplace could mean more productive employees and therefore an increase in customer satisfaction, or sales, for example.

This increase might be very hard to quantify, and it will depend on who your sponsor or signatories are, as to the level of detail they are expecting to see in this area.

Just because your benefit is not tangible does not mean that it should not be included.

As has been my message throughout this book what we are looking for here are REAL benefits. They must be measurable and attainable.

You are better to have only defined four or five substantial benefits of delivering this project than dozens that are unclear and not measurable nor achievable.

Your sponsor and signatories will be happier with clearly defined measurable and achievable benefits if they are realistic and not over inflated or made up

**Measuring Return on Investment via the benefits**

The whole aim of providing clear and measurable benefits are so that during the life of the project you can track deliverables ensuring that any changes you make to scope do not adversely impact the benefits.

This if often a problem with a business case that is not clear to start out with, or one where the project is not tracked against the business case. The scope then becomes so far from the original business case that it is no wonder there is a cost and time blow out.

Your signatories need to clear see that the benefits of approving this project add up to gains for the business which offsets the money they will spend. If this legitimate Return On Investment is not shown then the project should not be approved. Simple!

# TIP 6 – LIST THE BENEFITS

*Remember that benefits can be tangible (those things you can touch and are real) or intangible (those things that are unable to be physically touched, but things that are just as worthwhile).*

*Try to convert intangible benefits to tangible by accurate prediction of their potential benefit.*

# 11. The importance of documenting your risks

I know that I keep taking you 'back to basics'. I see value in ensuring that we are all on the same page when I am explaining things that need to be completed.

So, let's now look at the definition of a 'risk' as this is where we need to start:

- ◈ The Oxford English Dictionaries define risk as "expose (someone or something valued) to danger, harm or loss; Act in such a way as to bring about the possibility of (an unpleasant or unwelcome event)."

- ◈ The Chambers 21st Century Dictionary defines risk as "the chance or possibility of suffering loss, injury, damage, etc.; danger."

If you then look at the context of why you are writing your business case and what opportunity you are trying to build on, what exposure to loss, harm or damage might you face?

It is crucial to <u>list any risks</u> that you have identified in creating this business case.

Be sure to document any and all risks that you find, even at this early stage.

The next page contains a strategy for identifying your risks that you might find useful. I have found that it helps me identify risks that I might not otherwise have thought of.

By documenting these now, in the business case, I allow my key stakeholders and signatories to determine if there is too much risk in continuing with approval for the project.

This section is, therefore, invaluable to the overall decision-making process if it is written well.

# A strategy for identifying your risks

You might like to look at each of the following areas to identify risks:-

1. People – Are the right resources available?

2. Process – How will the proposed change impact other people and other processes?

3. Legal – Are they any legal or regulatory ramifications?

4. Financial – If we do not deliver this on time is there a risk to your funding?

5. Market – Are their changes in the marketplace that will impact negatively on what we want to achieve?

6. Technology – How stable is the future of your proposed technology solution?

7. Timing – If you do not meet the delivery timelines, does the benefit evaporate?

It may be valuable also to consider risks that are connected to each of the options that you have proposed. If there is more risk with a particular option, highlight this.

The more thorough you are here, the easier it will be to have a sound go / no-go decision made on approving the business case and to then start your project off on an excellent footing with risks identified and mitigation strategies in place.

Remember also to call out the risk or risks of not doing what you are proposing.

Some people think this is a bit too obvious, but I see it as necessary to show your sponsor that you are switched on and understand the implications and risks associated with not doing anything about the business problem you are calling out or the opportunity that is going to be missed.

If the risk of not fixing this issue is that you will continue to lose business to your competitors slowly, your sponsor/signatories need to know this. Again this sort of information helps them to weigh up the need to approve what it is that you are asking for, and having the best possible picture of the 'why' behind your business case.

Remember also to include the risks associated with the options that you are proposing. Give serious consideration to risks associated with each option as it may make the difference between something being a viable option and not.

## Document your risk mitigation strategies

Take the time to consider your risk mitigation strategies and document these too.

Your mitigation strategy should explain what you need to do to have the risk you have listed, not materialise or managed if it does. What planning and preparation would need to be in place and importantly who would need to be involved in any mitigation activity?

This mitigation work might highlight the need for additional resources that have a cost and time impact and need to be included in your business case. It is, therefore, critical to have thought through this, while preparing your business case.

You might consider that the time that you need to take to do this work now is a waste of time. On the contrary, I have found that the time I spend up front in detailing these risks and their mitigation strategies makes managing the project a lot easier and saves time overall.

It does not mean that further risks will not be captured as part of project delivery. It does mean that the right risk profile is attached to the project at an organisational level and this is important to ensure that delivery is going to provide the best business outcome. After all, isn't that what you are wanting to achieve in preparing this business case?

---

## TIP 7 – DOCUMENT RISKS AND THEIR MITIGATION STRATEGY(S)

*Is there a risk in not doing what you are proposing? If so, then call it out. Be sure to include risk mitigation strategies for any risks that you identify. You will show your sponsor/signatory that you are serious.*

---

# 12. What do your financials look like?

It is important to obtain high-level <u>realistic</u> cost estimates for each of the options being proposed in Net Present Value (NPV) terms. This realistic cost estimate will help to weigh up the viability of each of the options.

'Realistic' is the key word here. All too often the cost estimations in a business case are too 'ballpark' which means that when it comes time to deliver the project what you thought was going to cost $500,000, in fact, costs $1.5 Million (as in 'out of the ballpark'). Having large project cost overrun is not a good outcome for your business sponsor, or you.

If you are doing any IT system work as part of any option or proposal, it is important to have IT Architects involved in this phase of your business case preparation. I would expect them to have a clear understanding of the types of technology that are in the marketplace and what may work at an enterprise level for you. They will also have a reasonably good idea what costs would be associated with using different technologies. If not, then they will be able to find out.

Take the time to obtain quotes from external vendors, if applicable. (Remember my caveat about privacy of information here). It is important to get more than one competitive quote so that you are providing the best cost option to your sponsor. Be sure to follow any competitive quoting process that your organisation has within its procurement guidelines.

To do this, you need to be clear about the scope of what it is that you want the vendor to do. Most of the time you will have a good idea of the type of work that you need them to undertake, and they should, therefore, be able to provide you with a reasonably realistic quote.

The more pre-work that you do here on clarification and scoping, the more rigorous your overall outcome is going to be. Creating clarity of the scope may not mean creating full blown business requirements but if you have the time, develop them. It does mean having enough understanding to explain what you do and don't want to be included in your scope of work.

Developing business requirements is another time saver for your project. The time that it takes to develop quality business requirements here will save you time and money across the life of your overall project.

Your aim is to be so clear on your scope by the time you have completed writing your business case, that what's in, what's out and the assumptions you have made will be clear. Documenting all of these means you will be able to run your project with your eyes shut, well almost!

If the business cannot be clear about their problem and their needs when you start to define them for the solution, then don't undertake the project. Go to you sponsor and tell them you do not have the clarity that is needed to continue.

**Different type of costs**

Stop and look at the bigger picture of what it is going to cost to deliver this change entirely. Ensure that you have captured **all** costs in your financial estimates. Note that I have said, "deliver this change."

Developing cost estimates from a narrow view of the project is detrimental to the business and sets you up for project failure, even before you start.

You must look at what is required to implement this change holistically. What exactly do I mean by that? Who needs to be involved in making the transition successful, what do they need to do and how much is it going to cost.

Some different costs to consider:

- Change management costs
- Process re-engineering costs
- Legal costs
- Marketing material costs
- Ongoing software licence costs
- Data manipulation and migration costs
- Staff movement and relocation costs
- Dependent system hardware upgrade costs
- Training costs
- Telephony or other system change costs

There are many more costs here that may need to be included; this is just a sample to get you thinking about things in a different light. I often find that these are the costs that are forgotten when developing financials for a business case.

Is there after hours or weekend work required where the pay scale is different?

Do you need additional specialists to be available for the project (who are not part of a vendor's project team)?

If you go back to any end to end process diagrams (yes, note I said end to end), and look at what will be changing as part of this project delivery what is required for that to be successful?  Maybe everyone needs a new monitor; Maybe people need his or her telephone re-routed; Think outside the square, your immediate vision of what you think is required and get down into the detail.

It is the little things that are needed where the costs for implementation add up.  These are the things that will throw your budget way off track if there are too many of them that you have not captured now.

## Include contingency

Does your organisation have a policy about the inclusion of contingency?  Do you know what it is?  It is worthwhile asking this question.

Some organisations are very particular about it being a certain percentage of the total project spend.  Others want it down to exact dollar amounts.  Others will use a high-level ballpark percentage figure plus or minus.

Don't go down the path of estimating it, until you have checked if there is a policy in place regarding its calculation.  Finding out on way or the other will save you time in the long run.

## How to include contingency

It is okay to include a contingency in your cost estimates but be clear about it. List this as a separate cost item in your financials.  By listing the contingency requirements the sponsor/signatory approving your business case can see the total funding you are requesting. They may also want to see how it is calculated too. Be prepared to speak to this if you are questioned about it.

Any contingency should be identified as a risk, so be sure to add this to your list of risks.

You may find that if your contingency is too high, your sponsor or signatory may want you to obtain further information or to refine the scope and therefore the cost estimates.

## TIP 8 – GET HIGH LEVEL REALISTIC ESTIMATES

Do what it takes to get realistic costings. Request quotes from external vendors if necessary. Understand what is and isn't out of scope so that your estimates are for work that would deliver what is required.

# 13. Provide a high-level timeline for delivery of your chosen option

Your sponsor and the signatories approving your business case want to see that you have a good idea of how long it is going to take to deliver what you are making as your recommendation.

It is valuable to put a high-level Gantt chart in your business case with the details showing how you are going to phase the delivery of this recommended option (if that is needed).

For an IT delivery project, this would, of course, follow standard waterfall or Agile methods.

For business related projects consider how you would chunk up the work that needs to be undertaken so that you have checkpoints or gates to show you are progressing and can validate your cost estimates against the business case during delivery.

If you consider it valuable to add weight to options that are not viable you could also provide high-level timelines for these too.  These need not be in the form of Gantt charts, but a more pictorial representation.

It is valuable to put key milestones on the Gantt chart as indicative of how the project would be run. This view of the project allows your sponsor or signatories to validate if they feel there are enough checkpoints or gates during project delivery.

Also, remember to add in the resourcing requirements. The resource estimate can be at a high level with the type of resources required, e.g. developer, business SME, only.

Your Gantt chart should also show any critical dependencies, necessary for delivery against the suggested timeline.

Any work you do on developing a project schedule here can be used when you gain approval for your project to go ahead. So it will not be wasted.

*TIP 9 – INCLUDE A HIGH-LEVEL PROJECT TIMELINE FOR YOUR RECOMMENDED OPTION*

*Show your sponsor/signatory how long it is going to take to deliver your project. How long do they need to wait to see the problem solved or the opportunity materialise?*

# 14. Document your assumptions

It is paramount that your assumptions are recorded in your business case. Why? Documenting your assumptions allows your sponsor and signatories to sit in your shoes when deciding if they will approve your business case.

It is the equivalent of them being able to validate the story that you have told or developed. You might be writing about one story, and a signatory may know it as something completely different.

By documenting your assumptions, it creates openness about your information gathering process. It also helps in building trust. Trust is valuable moving into project delivery.

The assumptions allow them to fully understand what has and hasn't been factored into the cost estimates, the resourcing and the timeline for the options that you have documented. Remember to list **all** of your assumptions.

Here are just a few examples of assumptions:

- dependency on the latest software upgrade to the servers being deployed before the commencement of the build phase;

- resources currently on other projects be released by a certain date to start work immediately on the initial phase of this project;

- funding is available from this financial year's budget;

- funding will not be available in next financial year's budget;

- Legislation requiring the implementation of this proposal will pass parliament in the next six months.

You might have noted some assumptions that you captured during your options brainstorming session. Be sure to include these here too.

Assumptions should also spell out any dependencies that exist as a requirement of delivery.

# TIP 10 – REMEMBER TO LIST ALL YOUR ASSUMPTIONS

*Document all your assumptions. Documenting your assumptions makes it clear what has and hasn't been taken into consideration in preparing your business case.*

## 15. Make a recommendation

Your sponsor and signatories are going to want to know what you are recommending as the preferred way to handle the resolution of their need by issuing this business case and why you are recommending it.

At this point in your business case, if you have prepared it with the right level of detail included, it should be obvious why you are making the recommendation that you are.

If this is not the case, then I suggest you go back and look at the area's where your information provision is thin.

### Explaining why you are rejecting options

It is also very worthwhile explaining in a short and concise way why you are not recommending the other proposed options.

By doing this your sponsor and signatories can see your reasoning behind rejecting the other options. In its way, this also helps to strengthen the case for your recommended option.

Your case for not choosing an option needs to be based on actual evidence, for example:

- ◈ this option is going to take too long to deliver;

- ◈ this option has too many risks associated with it (you having called them out in your business case);

- ◈ this option is going to cost too much, and there is a cheaper more cost effective alternative;

- ◈ this option is of a strategic nature, and the business requires a tactical option to meet its current needs sooner.

# TIP 11 – MAKE A RECOMMENDATION

*Provide details for your sponsor or signatories as to which is your preferred option and why. Your case as to why you have chosen this as the recommended option needs to be strong. Also, remember to explain why you have rejected the other proposed options.*

## 16. Validate your case

### Stick to the facts

A business case is not the place to write a story. It is about facts delivered in a concise way to put the case as to why the problem you are discussing or the opportunity you are proposing needs consideration and how you would go about it.

It must contain the facts of what your problem is and why you need to resolve it, what will happen if you do not resolve it, what options you have for resolution and the cost to implement these. Stick to the facts.

If an opportunity is presented to the business, why do you need them to take it up, what is the benefit of doing so, and what is the value to the business of taking up the opportunity.

If you do this and provide a short and detailed business case, it will make the decision making easier, and you have a better chance of busy sponsors and signatories giving your business case a good hearing.

## Does your business case stack up?

If you have followed the tips outlined in this book, then you should now be at the point of knowing whether your business case is going to stack up and be well received.

If your business case does not stack up, then consider why it does not. What isn't right? Where do you lack information? Is the cost to implement the recommended solution going to outweigh the benefits? Remember, this may not be a problem for your sponsor.

Look at each of the areas within your business case and determine what needs to change, if possible. Is additional information required to have each person reading your document, able to make a yes or no decision quickly?

You need to be able to read it through and feel that you would support giving it a yes or no, yourself. If you cannot, then your signatories will not. Reading the document through this way is a real litmus test for validating it.

Once you have a solid draft, it is a good time to present your business case for review to your key stakeholders or signatories. Right back at the start of developing it, we spoke about getting them on board and understanding their needs for signing off your business case. Now it is time to test if you have delivered.

Take your draft business case to them to review. Getting your signatories comments will provide you with a temperature check before you send it up for final sign off and approval.

## Stopping the project before it starts

Early on in your information gathering, you may realise that the business case you are writing is not going to stack up. It not 'stacking up' may mean that it may not be worth taking it any further.

Go back to your sponsor and explain that in working up your business case you have realised that it does not appear to stack up. Let them read it through and see if they agree with you. They may have other suggestions.

By doing this, you are validating your thinking. There might be information that you are missing, that your sponsor might be aware of, which will make the difference. However, if in the end, it does not stack up, then this is a good outcome. It shows that you are not wasting your time and theirs on a proposal that will fail.

There is real value in not starting poorly conceived projects.

*Keep your business case short – but include all of the information needed for a decision*

A business case does not need to be the size of 'War and Peace'. It may only be a few pages, as long as it contains the right level of detailed information to match the scope of the project and for those signing it off to make an informed decision.

Naturally, the size of your business case (number of pages) will depend on what it is that you are hoping to achieve through business case approval.

It is not about the number of pages but more the quality and relevance of the information that is important.

### Don't create a marketing document – this is not about selling anything

Your business case should not be a marketing document or a sales pitch; you are not selling anything. It is not your place to run a marketing campaign for something that you see as a 'nice to have'.

It must be a succinct 'case' document setting out what the problem or opportunity is and how you are aiming to mitigate/achieve it.

Too many unnecessary words are only going to set your approvers off side and have them disregard your document.

# TIP 12 – VALIDATE YOUR CASE

*Minimise your story, stick to the facts. You are not marketing anything. Keep it succinct and ensure you include all the necessary information for an informed decision to be made. Validate if it stacks up. If it does not, what can you improve, or what is missing?*

# CHECKLIST FOR VALIDATING YOUR BUSINESS CASE

Problem or opportunity statement clearly identified

Yes/No

Are your requirements clearly documented (creates

scope clarity)                                Yes/No

Viable options proposed? (short and long term

considerations)                               Yes/No

Realistic funding needs identified            Yes/No

Realistic timeframes for delivery specified   Yes/No

Risks and Assumptions called out              Yes/No

-----------------------------------------------------------------------

Viable Option (your recommendation) provided

Yes/No

OR

No Go Option clear and project determined as Not

Viable                                        Yes/No

# 17. Conclusion

By following this process, you should have developed a strong business case that will maximise your chances of support from your sponsor and signatories.

Every business case is different. Every organisation is different. The process of putting together a business case need not be that different.

Get it right, and you have a better chance of getting the best outcome for the company – a project that is going to make a difference to your organisation, and you.

Develop a quality business case, and you are setting any project up for success by providing the strong foundation that it needs.

Good luck

## About the Author

Karen Cherrett is an experienced and qualified Project and Change Manager who has spent over twenty five years working on, or managing projects. In her roles supporting projects she has written and reviewed many business cases. Her approach is to write a business case that is the foundation of a project so that it is the benchmark for project delivery. She sees a business case as being the strongest foundation for a successful project. In this book Karen shares her expertise on what makes a strong business case and provides a step by step process to follow.

# Acknowledgements

I want to thank Malcolm Munro for his support in questioning my thinking and as my proofreader, and Lachlan Munro for challenging me when he did not understand what I was saying.

To the Senior Managers that I have worked with throughout my career who have helped me see the value of a Business case – thank you.

To Hilary for working with me on developing the best business case possible, thank you. It gave me insights into what makes a strong business case.

I also want to thank all the people who have visited my blog at projectmanagementinsight.com to read my posts on how to write a good business case – you gave me the inspiration for this book.

www.ingramcontent.com/pod-product-compliance
Lightning Source LLC
Chambersburg PA
CBHW050513210326
41521CB00011B/2441